When Satan Tells the Truth

Sweet Little Lies

KOLLIN L. TAYLOR

Editor
Valerie (@editor_valerie) of FIVERR

Cover Design
Les (GermanCreative) of FIVERR

Cover Photograph
"Julie" by Kollin L. Taylor

When Satan Tells the Truth

When Satan Tells the Truth

DEDICATION

To Valerie, whose selfless sacrifices helped me tremendously in navigating this hectic season of my life, thank you for everything. You are worthy to be praised (Proverbs 31:30-31).

CONTENTS

ACKNOWLEDGMENTS

Heavenly Father, You are a Man of Your Word; You faithfully watch over Your Words to perform Them. I never imagined the dream where You foretold a season of me writing fervently meant writing this tenth book in seven months. Ministers have preached and asked this question: "Can God trust you with trouble?" I shockingly profess that I am grateful for the troubles You have entrusted me with. Now, after giving me the grace to endure many afflictions at the enemy's hands, You have given me opportunities to expose him and his evil ways. Thank You for these opportunities to warn Your children. Most important, thank You for sending Your Holy Spirit to help me in writing this book, for the glory of Your Son, the LORD Jesus Christ.

PROLOGUE

Why would I write a book about Satan telling the truth if Jesus said:

*Ye are of your father the Devil, and the lusts of your father ye will do. He was a murderer from the beginning, and abode not in the truth, because **THERE IS NO TRUTH IN HIM. When he speaketh a lie, he speaketh of his own: for he is a liar, and the father of it.*** ~ John 8:44

The LORD is correct that the Devil is a liar and the father of lies. But a part of Satan's cunning is that he is not as divorced from the truth as many people may think. He is a seducer and a deceiver who will use the truth IF it serves his purpose. After all, it is hard to deceive some people with outright lies, which is why Satan will use sweet lies or even the truth.
The Apostle Paul warned:

Lest Satan should get an advantage of us: for we are not ignorant of his devices. ~ 2 Corinthians 2:11

When Satan Tells the Truth: Sweet Little Lies exposes the ultimate cover for the Devil, which is to use the truth against those who will not fall for his lies. Let us take a journey to see the ways how Satan attempts to use the truth to achieve his SINister agendas.

CHAPTER 1

THE FIRST TRUTH

It is well known that Satan deceived Eve in the Garden of Eden. But what is oft overlooked is that he used the truth to do so. Satan, the seducer, is more effective when he does not use an outright lie. This is why his words may sound good, even though his motives are corrupt. Please note what he said to Eve that made her look at the fruit of the Tree of the Knowledge of Good and Evil, to see that it was good to eat:

Now the serpent was more subtil than any beast of the field which the LORD God had made.
And he said unto the woman, Yea, hath God said, Ye shall not eat of every tree of the garden?
And the woman said unto the serpent, We may eat of the fruit of the trees of the garden: But of the fruit of the tree which is in the midst of the garden, God hath said, Ye shall not eat of it, neither shall ye touch it, lest ye die.
And the serpent said unto the woman, Ye shall not surely die:
For God doth know that in the day ye eat thereof, then YOUR EYES SHALL BE OPENED, and ye shall be as gods, knowing good and evil.

And when the woman saw that the tree was good for food, and that it was pleasant to the eyes, and a tree to be desired to make one wise, she took of the fruit thereof, and did eat, and gave also unto her husband with her; and he did eat.
And the eyes of them both were opened, *and they knew that they were naked; and they sewed fig leaves together, and made themselves aprons.* ~ Genesis 3:1-7

IF Eve knew what death was, Satan was correct in that neither she nor Adam dropped dead immediately after disobeying the Word of the LORD. Satan also said their eyes would be opened, and they certainly were. This is where some people get caught in the Devil's snares because he can deliver on what he says—at least some of the time and to an extent. What Satan is seldom truthful about are the consequences for people coming into agreement with him. Adam and Eve discovered the consequences of listening to Satan when God appeared and dealt with them for disobeying Him.

To show that Satan is not the liar most people think of him as, pay attention to what the LORD said after judging them. This shows that Satan's deception was based on the truth, but it was a truth that God did not intend for Adam and Eve to learn:

And the LORD God said, Behold, ***THE MAN IS BECOME AS ONE OF US, to know good and evil****: and now, lest he put forth his hand, and take also of the Tree of Life, and eat, and live for ever:*
Therefore the LORD God sent him forth from the Garden of Eden, to till the ground from whence he was taken.
So He drove out the man; and He placed at the east of the Garden of Eden Cherubims, and a flaming sword which turned every way, to keep the way of the Tree of Life. ~ Genesis 3:22-24

Satan did not point them to the Tree of Life, which would have been more beneficial for Adam and Eve, but he spoke the truth about the Tree of the Knowledge of Good and Evil. Even though created in His image and likeness, the LORD God confirmed Satan's words that if Eve were to eat from the tree, her eyes would be opened, and she would know good and evil. She would become like God.

Because Adam followed Eve, his eyes were also opened to that knowledge that the LORD wanted them to avoid. There was also truth to Satan's words that they would not die, at least not immediately. However, that does not mean God had lied; His Words were true, but They did not have the immediate effect people would expect. There are times when God's Words have immediate effects, but they are not always immediately noticed. For example, after their eyes were opened, the LORD God called for Adam, but he and his wife were hiding from Him. That represents a death in their relationship with God to where they had started hiding from Him. Also, because of their rebellion against God, they went from being naked and unashamed to hiding from each other (Genesis 2:25).

It is believed that Satan convinced a third of the LORD God's angels to join him. If he had told them that they would be like God, that is also correct to a degree. The truth behind gods such as Baal, Dagon, Molech, Ashtoreth, Chemosh, and Milcom is they have idols to represent them, but behind those idols are devils, Satan's fallen angels. That is why those who serve other gods may have spiritual powers that are based on their relationship with and sacrifices to those gods.

Many Scriptures indicate that behind those gods and their representative idols are devils. One such example came from Moses, who spoke of that fact:

They provoked Him [Yahweh] *to jealousy with strange gods, with abominations provoked they Him to anger.*

> *They sacrificed unto devils, not to God; to gods whom they knew not, to new gods that came newly up, whom your fathers feared not.*
> ~ Deuteronomy 32:16-17

The angels who rebelled with Satan may enjoy godlike status, but that will end around the time of the fulfillment of Revelation 19. If Satan told some of the LORD's angels, that by following him, they would be like God, which was a part of his original aspirations, he would have been correct (Isaiah 14:12-21). In fact, even Satan is known as a god, as Paul wrote:

> *But if our Gospel be hid, it is hid to them that are lost: In whom **the god of this world** hath blinded the minds of them which believe not, lest the Light of the glorious Gospel of Christ, who is the image of God, should shine unto them.* ~ 2 Corinthians 4:3-4

Most likely, Satan will not specify that ruling with him is temporary and will be followed by God's severe but just judgment of everlasting sufferings (Revelation 20:10-15). On the contrary, reigning with Christ Jesus has everlasting good fruit (2 Timothy 2:11-12).

Satan, the deceiver, knows that sometimes his most effective tool for deception is the truth. People are more inclined to follow him if he tells them the truth. That is because they will not detect any lies to deter their compliance. He hopes that by the time they get to the lies, it will be too late for them. Therefore, in the fight against Satan, it is not only important to discern the truth, but we must also, with the Holy Spirit's help, discern who is communicating the truth to us and the motive behind it.

Particularly because we have the Bible and can doublecheck to see if words are the Words of God, it is important to discern that the Word of God is coming from the Spirit of God. That factors into when Paul wrote:

I marvel that ye are so soon removed from Him that called you into the grace of Christ unto another gospel: Which is not another; but there be some that trouble you, and would pervert the Gospel of Christ.
*But though we, **or an angel from heaven**, preach any other gospel unto you than that which we have preached unto you, let him be accursed.*
As we said before, so say I now again, if any man preach any other gospel unto you than that ye have received, let him be accursed. ~ Galatians 1:6-9

A tragic part of that Scripture is that it points to people who will follow another gospel, a way that seems right to people but will lead to death. It will seem holy and honoring to the LORD, but will be based on doctrines of devils that Paul also cautioned about:

*Now the Spirit speaketh expressly, that in the latter times **some shall depart from the faith, giving heed to SEDUCING SPIRITS, and DOCTRINES OF DEVILS**; Speaking lies in hypocrisy; having their conscience seared with a hot iron; Forbidding to marry, and commanding to abstain from meats, which God hath created to be received with thanksgiving of them which believe and know the truth.*
For every creature of God is good, and nothing to be refused, if it be received with thanksgiving: For it is sanctified by the Word of God and prayer.
~ 1 Timothy 4:1-5

Doctrines of Devils are based on the Word of God. The holiness they project may even seem like the embodiment of when Jesus said:

Be ye therefore perfect, even as your Father which is in heaven is perfect. ~ Matthew 5:48

Sadly, because such things are based on the doctrines of devils, their righteousness aligns more with when Jesus proclaimed:

But woe unto you, scribes and Pharisees, hypocrites! For ye shut up the KINGdom of Heaven against men: for ye neither go in yourselves, neither suffer ye them that are entering to go in.
Woe unto you, scribes and Pharisees, hypocrites! For ye devour widows' houses, and for a pretence make long prayer: therefore ye shall receive the greater damnation.
Woe unto you, scribes and Pharisees, hypocrites!
For ye compass sea and land to make one proselyte, and when he is made, YE MAKE HIM TWOFOLD MORE THE CHILD OF HELL THAN YOURSELVES...
...Woe unto you, scribes and Pharisees, hypocrites! For ye make clean the outside of the cup and of the platter, but within they are full of extortion and excess.
Thou blind Pharisee, cleanse first that which is within the cup and platter, that the outside of them may be clean also.
Woe unto you, scribes and Pharisees, hypocrites!
FOR YE ARE LIKE UNTO WHITED SEPULCHRES, WHICH INDEED APPEAR BEAUTIFUL OUTWARD, but are within full of dead men's bones, and of all uncleanness.
EVEN SO YE ALSO OUTWARDLY APPEAR RIGHTEOUS UNTO MEN, but within ye are full of hypocrisy and iniquity. ~ Matthew 23:13-15, 25-28

Satan forms religious organizations where the people may seem like the holiest on earth, sometimes covered from head to toe. But the sad truth is that they are further away from the LORD than many people can imagine. Satan's success in this form of deception lies in strict adherence to the Scriptures, the Word of God, but it is void of the Spirit of God, and as Jesus said, the Holy Spirit is the Spirit of Truth who guides us into ALL Truth (John 16:12-15).

Unfortunately, victims of such deception are repeating the sins of others, about whom Jesus said:

*"Well did Isaiah prophesy of you hypocrites, as it is written, **'This people honors Me with their lips, but their heart is far from Me; in vain do they worship Me,** teaching as doctrines the commandments of men.'*
You leave the Commandment of God and hold to the tradition of men."
And He said to them, "You have a fine way of rejecting the Commandment of God in order to establish your tradition! ~ Mark 7:6-9 (ESV)

That is why the LORD also gave this shocking commentary:

Not every one that saith unto Me, LORD, LORD, shall enter into the KINGdom of Heaven; but he that doeth the will of My Father which is in heaven.
Many will say to Me in that day, LORD, LORD, have we not prophesied in Thy name?
And in Thy name have cast out devils?
And in Thy name done many wonderful works?
*And then will I profess unto them, **I NEVER knew you:** depart from Me, ye that work iniquity.*
~ Matthew 7:21-23

IF you are versed in the Scriptures, you may have noticed something that the LORD said that may have seemingly invalidated this book's premise of Satan telling the truth. How can anyone who cast out devils not make it into heaven? After all, Jesus spoke of the unity in Satan's kingdom that may make it seem as if anyone who casts out devils is a child of God:

Then was brought unto Him one possessed with a devil, blind, and dumb: and He healed him, insomuch that the blind and dumb both spake and saw.
And all the people were amazed, and said, Is not this the son of David?
*But when the Pharisees heard it, they said, **This fellow doth not cast out devils, but by Beelzebub the prince of the devils.***
*And Jesus knew their thoughts, and said unto them, **Every kingdom divided against itself is brought to desolation; and every city or house divided against itself shall not stand: AND IF SATAN CAST OUT SATAN, HE IS DIVIDED AGAINST HIMSELF; HOW SHALL THEN HIS KINGDOM STAND?***
And if I by Beelzebub cast out devils, by whom do your children cast them out?
Therefore they shall be your judges.
But if I cast out devils by the Spirit of God, then the KINGdom of God is come unto you.
Or else how can one enter into a strong man's house, and spoil his goods, except he first bind the strong man? And then he will spoil his house. ~ Matthew 12:22-29

Devils know how to put on a show, including feigning deliverance. For example, a devil may pretend to leave, such as by mimicking the actions of the devil Jesus cast out of a young man (Mark 9:25-27). But instead of leaving, the devil simply remains dormant for a while before resuming the torments. In other cases, the devil(s) may leave the person's body but reenter the next time its former host goes to sleep.

The above deceptions almost demand that Satan tells the truth, including admitting that Jesus is LORD as he points a way to get to Him, which is where the lies lie. Satan must present compelling evidence to give the illusion that when he starts a religious organization, he is leading people to Christ. The church is not going to have an image of Jesus with devil's horns. Satan must use the truth to make the lies as undetectable as possible so that those who are deceived do not realize it; as a result, they will evangelize for Satan in Jesus's name.

CHAPTER 2

THE SEDUCTIVE TRUTH

When Satan tried tempting Jesus after His baptism, the LORD had numerous potential responses to rebuke the Devil. Interestingly, despite his wildest assertions, such as in this exchange, the LORD never called Satan a liar:

> *And the Devil, taking Him up into an high mountain, shewed unto Him all the kingdoms of the world in a moment of time.*
> *And the Devil said unto Him, All this power will I give thee, and the glory of them: for that is delivered unto me; and to whomsoever I will I give it.*
> *IF thou therefore wilt worship me, all shall be thine.*
> ~ Luke 4:5-7

The Devil made a bold claim, but with the stipulation that Jesus, his Creator, would need to worship him. Instead of calling Satan a liar with no power to do such a thing, the LORD rebuked him with:

> *Get thee behind Me, Satan: for it is written, Thou shalt worship the LORD thy God, and Him only shalt thou serve.* ~ Luke 4:8

Again, Satan is the god of this world, and he has the power and authority to do things for those who serve him. Therefore, Jesus warned:

If any man will come after Me, let him deny himself, and take up his cross, and follow Me.
For whosoever will save his life shall lose it: and whosoever will lose his life for My sake shall find it.
For what is a man profited, if he shall gain the whole world, and lose his own soul?
Or what shall a man give in exchange for his soul?
For the Son of Man shall come in the glory of His Father with His angels; and then He shall reward every man according to his works. ~ Matthew 16:24-27

Satan will offer people the world, but it will cost them their souls and place with Jesus Christ. Unfortunately, many people have taken this bait from Satan and enjoyed a measure of carnal success. However, this comes with awful side effects during their service to him, often leading to tragic endings.

Oddly, some people think others are joking when they claim to have sold their souls to the Devil. But those who make such claims typically experience carnal "success" that drives others to envy. They also give hints, such as statements about serving Satan, flashing demonic hand signals, and other things to publicly profess their allegiance to Satan. In other words, they worship Satan, which is a requirement of their covenant with him, and they lead people in joining that worship, often under the guise of entertainment value. They tell the truth about the god they serve, such as in their clothing/costumes, set designs, and musical lyrics, yet many people still refuse to believe the truth that is in plain sight.

Eventually, Satan's worshippers typically start showing at least a hint of regret when they feel the impacts of their enslavement and experience the consequences of making deals with the Devil. Even though the LORD Jesus Christ can break those evil covenants, the signatories of such deals are made to feel as if they are unbreakable and inescapable. And for those who do not feel that way, the Devil uses this to keep them in bondage to him. Their evil works to form and maintain those covenants are weaponized to make them feel as if God would not accept them when that may not be the case. But many of the Bible's heroes, such as Moses, King David, and the Apostle Paul, had less than stellar records, yet the LORD still used them mightily for His glory.

You may have also noticed a person who grew up in a CHRISTian home, but to gain worldly success, does it the Devil's way. But upon recognizing the errant ways, they try to return to the LORD, possibly by doing works to seemingly glorify His name and professing Jesus as their LORD and Savior. But in some cases, the person goes back to the satanic ways and ends up worse than before. Sadly, instead of recognizing the Devil's pull on these people, sometimes Christians will accuse those individuals of feigning repentance instead of trying to help them escape from the Devil's clutches. If anyone feigns repentance, as if to mock God, He will never be mocked (Galatians 6:7-8). In addition, several Scriptures point to the dangers of not repenting. One of those is this powerful warning:

For if we sin wilfully after that we have received the knowledge of the Truth, there remaineth no more sacrifice for sins, but a certain fearful looking for of judgment and fiery indignation, which shall devour the adversaries. ~ Hebrews 10:26-27

But to you, I also say, do not be among those who push a person back into the Devil's arms because of your hardened heart, as if you are the one who determines who gets saved and who can call themselves Christians. Sometimes, professing Christians turn people away from wanting to be CHRISTians with their ungodly conduct that fails to glorify the Christ they profess to follow. Some people in the kingdom of darkness, with good reason, see Christians as being phonier than the Devil. Sometimes, the truth he tells is by being evil to them instead of pretending as if he is holy but is meanspirited.

Please keep in mind that Saul of Tarsus fought against CHRISTians in his perceived service to God, until Jesus corrected him (Acts 9). Appallingly, many Christians are committing a similar sin by trying to block the way to salvation for those who are legitimately seeking a relationship with the LORD Jesus Christ. Sure, by God's grace, let no one deceive you. But also, ensure that you do not fight against God as He tries to bring people into His KINGdom. Do not become like this Pharisee:

And He spake this parable unto certain which trusted in themselves that they were righteous, and despised others:
Two men went up into the Temple to pray; the one a Pharisee, and the other a publican.
The Pharisee stood and prayed thus with himself, God, I thank Thee, that I am not as other men are, extortioners, unjust, adulterers, or even as this publican. I fast twice in the week, I give tithes of all that I possess. And the publican, standing afar off, would not lift up so much as his eyes unto heaven, but smote upon his breast, saying, God be merciful to me a sinner.
I tell you, this man went down to his house justified rather than the other: for every one that exalteth himself shall be abased; and he that humbleth himself shall be exalted. ~ Luke 18:9-14

Sometimes, we believe that it is impossible for Satan to tell the truth to the point where when he does, we refuse to believe him. The same thing applies to those who serve him and truthfully confess that they sold their souls to him. Some CHRISTians get into the semantics that God said all souls are His, which means people cannot sell their souls to the Devil to discredit those confessions

(Ezekiel 18:4). But please note that Jesus spoke of people *forfeiting* their souls. When people speak of selling their souls to the Devil, it ties back to when Jesus said, while referring to Himself as the One who will judge all of us:

Fear them not therefore: for there is nothing covered, that shall not be revealed; and hid, that shall not be known. What I tell you in darkness, that speak ye in light: and what ye hear in the ear, that preach ye upon the housetops.
And fear not them which kill the body, but are not able to kill the soul: but rather fear Him which is able to destroy both soul and body in hell. ~ Matthew 10:26-28

Despite its severity, the Scripture is also an inspiration for those who are trying to escape from the Devil's grasp, but he is using fear to keep them in bondage to him. Fear God, and only Him.

A part of the Devil's fear-based system is to threaten people's lives, whether the person who made a covenant with him or the life of someone that person loves. He may certainly be able to deliver on such threats, which is a part of him telling the truth at times. Satan attempted to end Jesus's life, but he did so covertly after Jesus refused to bow and worship him. In this next move, Satan tried to use the Scriptures to end Jesus's life:

And he brought Him to Jerusalem, and set Him on a pinnacle of the Temple, and said unto Him, If thou be the Son of God, cast thyself down from hence:
For it is written, He shall give His angels charge over thee, to keep thee: And in their hands they shall bear thee up, lest at any time thou dash thy foot against a stone.
And Jesus answering said unto him, It is said, Thou shalt not tempt the LORD thy God.
And when the Devil had ended all the temptation, he departed from Him for a season. ~ Luke 4:9-13

Without getting overly caught up on it not being a verbatim quote as the Scripture is written, the Devil did not lie when he quoted Psalm 91:11-12 to Jesus, which reads:

For He shall give His angels charge over thee, to keep thee in all thy ways.
They shall bear thee up in their hands, lest thou dash thy foot against a stone.

That shows how the Devil truthfully uses the Word of God to deceive people. But it validates why Jesus said this about and to His followers:

My sheep hear My voice, and I know them, and they follow Me: And I give unto them eternal life; and they shall never perish, neither shall any man pluck them out of My hand. ~ John 10:27-28

The LORD said His sheep hear His voice instead of His Words. That is because Satan can quote Jesus's Words and even mimic His voice, but Jesus's sheep must know His voice. I will explore this in further detail in an upcoming chapter.

Many people will come in the LORD's name, and some will not, but despite how things may seem or sound, they are messengers of Satan. They may tell the truth, but they are of the wrong spirit. Despite their professed or seeming servitude to the LORD, they are children of the Devil who are doing his will and works, sometimes covertly. They are wolves in sheep's clothing or wolves in shepherd's clothing. The words from their lips or fingertips are like what is written about this seductress:

My son, attend unto my wisdom, and bow thine ear to my understanding: That thou mayest regard discretion, and that thy lips may keep knowledge.

For the lips of a strange woman drop as an honeycomb, and her mouth is smoother than oil: But her end is bitter as wormwood, sharp as a two-edged sword.
Her feet go down to death; her steps take hold on hell.
Lest thou shouldest ponder the path of life, her ways are moveable, that thou canst not know them.
Hear me now therefore, O ye children, and depart not from the words of my mouth.
Remove thy way far from her, and come not nigh the door of her house: Lest thou give thine honour unto others, and thy years unto the cruel: Lest strangers be filled with thy wealth; and thy labours be in the house of a stranger; And thou mourn at the last, when thy flesh and thy body are consumed, And say, How have I hated instruction, and my heart despised reproof; And have not obeyed the voice of my teachers, nor inclined mine ear to them that instructed me! ~ Proverbs 5:1-13

Satan is known for his seductive, sweet little lies, but he also knows how to use the truth to his advantage. Remember, the Antichrist is of Satan, but he must convince people that he is the Christ.

CHAPTER 3

AN ANGEL OF LIGHT

Paul revealed that Satan masquerades as an angel of Light (2 Corinthians 11:13-15). That means he pulls on his former position of serving God, being in His presence, and being familiar with His ways to pretend as if he is still an angel of God. Brazenly, Satan sometimes masquerades as if he is God. I, along with many other people, have had dreams about Jesus, and something about his character revealed that it was a devil instead of the only begotten Son of God, the Messiah. That factors into why, when asked about the signs of the end of time, Jesus said:

> *Then if any man shall say unto you, Lo, here is Christ, or there; believe it not.*
> ***For there shall arise FALSE CHRISTS**, and false prophets, and shall shew great signs and wonders; insomuch that, if it were possible, they shall deceive the very elect.*
> *Behold, I have told you before.*
> *Wherefore if they shall say unto you, Behold, he is in the desert; go not forth: behold, he is in the secret chambers; believe it not.* ~ Matthew 24:23-26

Unfortunately, Thomas, also known as Didymus, took those Words so seriously that he refused to believe the other apostles and disciples when they told him of Jesus's resurrection. He refused to let anyone deceive him, especially after Judas, whom Jesus said was a devil, had covertly operated amongst them for years without them discerning his evil deeds and intentions. Therefore, when told of the LORD's resurrection and appearance, Didymus said:

Except I shall see in His hands the print of the nails, and put my finger into the print of the nails, and thrust my hand into His side, I will not believe. ~ John 20:25

Jesus made another appearance to His disciples and gave Didymus the opportunity to do those things. The LORD gently corrected him for his lack of faith in not believing the other disciples' TESTimonies:

Thomas, because thou hast seen Me, thou hast believed: blessed are they that have not seen, and yet have believed. ~ John 20:29

There are at least two reasons for the Devil to masquerade as an angel of Light. The first is many people would not serve him if they knew his identity, agenda, and the costs of serving him. When Satan tried Jesus, He knew exactly who He was dealing with and the deeper meanings behind his words. That was why Jesus referred to him as Satan. It is more difficult to get deceived when you know who you are dealing with.

When the LORD God warned Cain that sin was crouching at his door, but he must rule over him [sin], he disobeyed (Genesis 4:7). After the LORD God judged Cain for his disobedience, this was his response to that judgment:

My punishment is greater than I can bear.

~ Genesis 4:13

Remarkably, the Lord God referred to sin as "him" instead of "it." That meant sin was a person, which points to Satan, who was known as the angel Lucifer, about whom God said:

Thou art the anointed cherub that covereth; and I have set thee so: thou wast upon the holy mountain of God; thou hast walked up and down in the midst of the stones of fire.
Thou wast perfect in thy ways from the day that thou wast created, TILL INIQUITY WAS FOUND IN THEE.
*By the multitude of thy merchandise they have filled the midst of thee with violence, and **thou hast sinned**: therefore I will cast thee as profane out of the mountain of God: and I will destroy thee, O covering cherub, from the midst of the stones of fire.*
Thine heart was lifted up because of thy beauty, thou hast corrupted thy wisdom by reason of thy brightness: I will cast thee to the ground, I will lay thee before kings, that they may behold thee.
Thou hast defiled thy sanctuaries by the multitude of thine iniquities, by the iniquity of thy traffick; therefore will I bring forth a fire from the midst of thee, it shall devour thee, and I will bring thee to ashes upon the earth in the sight of all them that behold thee.
~ Ezekiel 28:14-18

I believe that many people will repeat Cain's words upon receiving their final judgment from God, and that includes Satan and his angels because their punishment will be more than they can bear. That reminds me of when the apostle wrote:

Beloved, think it not strange concerning the fiery trial which is to try you, as though some strange thing happened unto you: But rejoice, inasmuch as ye are partakers of Christ's sufferings; that, when His glory shall be revealed, ye may be glad also with exceeding joy.

If ye be reproached for the name of Christ, happy are ye; for the spirit of glory and of God resteth upon you: on their part He is evil spoken of, but on your part He is glorified.

But let none of you suffer as a murderer, or as a thief, or as an evildoer, or as a busybody in other men's matters.

Yet if any man suffer as a CHRISTian, let him not be ashamed; but let him glorify God on this behalf.

*For the time is come that judgment must begin at the house of God: and if it first begin at us, **what shall the end be of them that obey not the Gospel of God?***

~ 1 Peter 4:12-17

It is better to suffer now, as a CHRISTian, for Jesus's name, than how those who served Satan will suffer.

The other reason Satan masquerades as an angel of Light is to mislead people into thinking they are on the path of righteousness. He pretends to be an angel of Light so that people will not believe in the LORD Jesus Christ and the events that are pointing to His imminent return. Satan wants people to become complacent to either die in their sins or experience the LORD's return while still living in sin. Either way, Satan, as an angel of Light, gets to ensnare souls to have them cast into the pits of hell.

His deeds while masquerading as an angel of Light are meant to destroy people's faith, including where they will profess to be Bible-believing Christians, yet they refuse to believe the things of the Bible that happen around them. For example, they do not believe in the gifts of the Holy Spirit being in operation, according to 1 Corinthians 12:1-11. That includes the belief that the LORD Jesus does not need or use certain ministry gifts today because we have the Bible. Thus, a point of controversy is whether Jesus has prophets today. Critics often cite the prominence of false prophets, as warned about in 1 John 4:1. But they overlook the fact that there are Biblical examples of where the false prophets outnumbered the prophets of the LORD. Elijah faced 450 false prophets on Mount Carmel (1 Kings 18:20-40). Likewise, Micaiah later contended with 400 other false prophets (1 Kings 22). Even prophets of the LORD were accused of being false or self-appointed back then (Jeremiah 29:26-27). People say the LORD has no further use for prophets. But upcoming events about the LORD's two witnesses (prophets) who will prophesy for three-and-a-half years, say otherwise (Revelation 11:1-13).

The Devil wants people to harden their hearts to certain things, particularly spiritual things, which include hardening their hearts towards God. That factors into why Jesus said:

...When the Son of man cometh, shall He find faith on the earth? ~ Luke 18:8

Faith plays a major role in our relationship with the LORD, which is why the Scripture states:

But WITHOUT FAITH it is impossible to please Him: *for he that cometh to God must believe that He is, and that He is a rewarder of them that diligently seek Him.* ~ Hebrews 11:6

Satan knows the Word of God, which is why he uses It against people, including CHRISTians. The Devil also knows that the Word of God is a powerful weapon, which Paul referred to as *the sWORD of the Spirit* (Ephesians 6:17). In spiritual battles, he tries to use the weapon we were given to use against him to defeat us.

Satan also knows the power of doubt, such as what is written about this impediment in Jesus's ministry on earth:

And when He was come into His own country, He taught them in their synagogue, insomuch that they were astonished, and said, Whence hath this man this wisdom, and these mighty works?
Is not this the carpenter's son?
Is not his mother called Mary?
And his brethren, James, and Joses, and Simon, and Judas?
And his sisters, are they not all with us?
Whence then hath this man all these things?
And they were offended in Him.
But Jesus said unto them, A prophet is not without honour, save in his own country, and in his own house.
And He did not many mighty works there BECAUSE OF THEIR UNBELIEF. ~ Matthew 13:54-58

Their unbelief caused Jesus to move on to other places to glorify God with His mighty works and teachings.

As a masquerading angel of Light, the Devil gets to operate within the Body of Christ. And by even using the Word of God, he can convince people not to believe the things of God. It does not mean people who are deceived in such a way are going to hell. It simply means they may miss out on certain things in their relationship with the LORD, like when He told the Israelites to go and possess the Promised Land. But due to their unbelief, most of the men of the generation, age twenty and older, were kept out of that land because they listened to the voices of fear and doubt of ten of the spies whom Moses had sent to search the territory. The other two spies, Caleb and Joshua, had faith in the LORD and His promises. They were like two prophets of the LORD, who were outnumbered by ten who were not (Numbers 14). Interestingly, like when Satan operates as an angel of Light, the ten spies were telling the truth when they reported:

And there we saw the giants, the sons of Anak, which come of the giants: and we were in our own sight as grasshoppers, and so we were in their sight.
~ Numbers 13:33

The Israelites were undoubtedly facing giants, so it was the truth. However, those ten men had seemingly forgotten that they had God on their side and everything He had done to get them out of Egypt and away from the pursuing Egyptian army.

When Satan operates as an angel of Light, he sounds logical, a voice of reason to keep people safe, even when the LORD wants them to have faith in Him. Faith in the LORD is not always based on sight. An example is this interaction between Joshua and the Angel of the LORD, when God wanted him to lead the Israelites to conquer Jericho:

Now JERICHO WAS STRAITLY SHUT UP because of the children of Israel: none went out, and none came in.
And the LORD said unto Joshua, **See, I have given into thine hand Jericho, and the king thereof, and the mighty men of valour.**
And ye shall compass the city, all ye men of war, and go round about the city once.
Thus shalt thou do six days.
And seven priests shall bear before the ark seven trumpets of rams' horns: and the seventh day ye shall compass the city seven times, and the priests shall blow with the trumpets.
And it shall come to pass, that when they make a long blast with the ram's horn, and when ye hear the sound of the trumpet, all the people shall shout with a great shout; and the wall of the city shall fall down flat, and the people shall ascend up every man straight before him. ~ Joshua 6:1-5

Joshua had to look beyond the obvious and trust what the LORD had stated.

When Satan masquerades as an angel of Light, it is to covertly gain access to destroy a Believer from within, just like how Judas was a destroyer from within Jesus's inner circle of disciples.

CHAPTER 4

MESSENGERS OF SATAN

One of the reasons people do not discern the Devil's voice is because they hear or see the truth that he communicates. The same applies to those who serve Satan, such as Judas. Jesus did not call Judas out by name, but He was referring to him when He told His apostles that one of them was a devil (John 6:70-71). The apostles knew a wolf in shepherd's clothing was among them, but they were clueless about who that person was, even at what we call The Last Supper when Jesus said one of them would betray Him. None of the apostles said Judas had those intentions. Instead, they asked Jesus if they were the one. Even Judas turned to the LORD and said:

Master, is it I? ~ Matthew 26:25

This account is even more shocking because the other apostles still could not figure out who the devil was in their midst:

He then lying on Jesus' breast saith unto Him, **LORD,
who is it?**
*Jesus answered, He it is, to whom I shall give a sop,
when I have dipped it.*
**And when He had dipped the sop, He gave it to
Judas Iscariot, the son of Simon.**
And after the sop **Satan entered into him***.*
*Then said Jesus unto him, That thou doest, do quickly.
Now no man at the table knew for what intent He spake
this unto him.
For some of them thought, because Judas had the bag,
that Jesus had said unto him, Buy those things that we
have need of against the feast; or, that he should give
something to the poor.* ~ John 13:25-29

IF Judas was not a messenger of Satan before, he
certainly became one when the Devil entered the apostle.
Again, John asked Jesus who was the betrayer, Jesus
told the sign of who it would be, and the apostles still did
not know the answer. But a part of that stemmed from
Judas's words, which he truthfully spoke, but it was a
cover for his evil intentions:

*Then Jesus six days before the Passover came to
Bethany, where Lazarus was, which had been dead,
whom He raised from the dead.
There they made Him a supper; and Martha served: but
Lazarus was one of them that sat at the table with Him.
Then took Mary a pound of ointment of spikenard, very
costly, and anointed the feet of Jesus, and wiped His
feet with her hair: and the house was filled with the
odour of the ointment.*
**Then saith one of his disciples, Judas Iscariot,
Simon's son, which should betray Him, WHY WAS
NOT THIS OINTMENT SOLD FOR THREE HUNDRED
PENCE, AND GIVEN TO THE POOR?**

This he said, not that he cared for the poor; BUT BECAUSE HE WAS A THIEF, and had the bag, and bare what was put therein.
Then said Jesus, Let her alone: against the day of My burying hath she kept this. For the poor always ye have with you; but Me ye have not always. ~ John 12:1-8

To this day, like Judas, messengers of Satan use feigned concern for the poor and the less fortunate to cover their evil ways and deeds. Judas cared more about money than he did the poor, a sign of him being a covert messenger of Satan.

I wonder if, after the Passover seder, when Judas was out on his assignment and Jesus said these Words, any of the apostles knew whom He was referring to:

And now I AM no more in the world, but these are in the world, and I come to Thee.
Holy Father, keep through Thine own name those Whom Thou hast given Me, that they may be one, as We are.
While I was with them in the world, I kept them in Thy name: ***those that Thou gavest Me I have kept, and NONE OF THEM IS LOST, BUT THE SON OF PERDITION;*** *that the Scripture might be fulfilled.*
~ John 17:11-12

It was only at this time that we can say the apostles definitively knew who the son of hell was, the devil among them, whom Jesus had repeatedly warned them about:

When Jesus had spoken these Words, He went forth with His disciples over the brook Cedron, where was a garden, into the which He entered, and His disciples.
And Judas also, which betrayed Him, knew the place: for Jesus ofttimes resorted thither with His disciples.
Judas then, having received a band of men and officers from the chief priests and Pharisees, cometh thither with lanterns and torches and weapons.

Jesus therefore, knowing all things that should come upon Him, went forth, and said unto them, Whom seek ye?
They answered him, Jesus of Nazareth.
Jesus saith unto them, I AM He.
And Judas also, which betrayed Him, stood with them.
~ John 18:1-5

Judas was an antichrist who foreshadowed the Antichrist, who, if you can even begin to imagine, will be craftier than Judas. Likewise, when the Antichrist's identity is revealed, he will have done monumental damage, so much so that he and the false prophet will not appear before Jesus on Judgment Day; instead, this will be their judgment:

And the beast [Antichrist] was taken, and with him the false prophet that wrought miracles before him, with which he deceived them that had received the mark of the beast, and them that worshipped his image.
These both were CAST ALIVE into a lake of fire burning with brimstone. ~ Revelation 19:20

Things will not end well for unrepentant messengers of Satan.

Another of the Bible's messengers of Satan sounded like a prophetess, but note what she said while under the influence of an evil spirit:

*And it came to pass, as we went to prayer, **a certain damsel possessed with A SPIRIT OF DIVINATION** met us, which brought her masters much gain by soothsaying:*
The same followed Paul and us, and cried, saying,
These men are the servants of the Most High God, which shew unto us the way of salvation.
And this did she many days.

But Paul, being grieved, turned and said to the spirit, I command thee in the name of Jesus Christ to come out of her.
And he came out the same hour. ~ Acts 16:16-18

She, or more accurately, the spirit in her, told the truth. The spirit was preaching the truth about Paul and his cohort's ministries. However, even though the words were true, thanks to Paul's discernment from the Holy Spirit, he discerned that the truth was coming from an evil spirit. Therefore, Paul dealt with the evil spirit as the Holy Spirit inspired him to write for our edification and exhortation:

Take no part in the unfruitful works of darkness, but instead expose them. ~ Ephesians 5:11 (ESV)

Many people cannot fathom that the Devil and his servants would sink to such a low, to tell the truth about God. If we use the Word of God without the Spirit of God, we may get stuck and get caught off-guard by the Devil such as because this Scripture states:

Beloved, do not believe every spirit, but test the spirits to see whether they are from God, for many false prophets have gone out into the world.
*By this you know the Spirit of God: **every spirit that confesses that Jesus Christ has come in the flesh is from God,** and every spirit that does not confess Jesus is not from God. This is the spirit of the Antichrist, which you heard was coming and now is in the world already. ~ 1 John 4:1-3 (ESV)*

Please know that some evil spirits, even though it may be painful for them to admit it, will speak the truth about Jesus IF that is what it takes to deceive their intended victim. Never forget that while many religious leaders were questioning Jesus's Messiahship, He was having encounters with devils, such as this:

> *And devils also came out of many, crying out, and saying,* **Thou art Christ the Son of God.**
> *And He rebuking them suffered them not to speak: for they knew that He was Christ.* ~ Luke 4:41

Please let that simmer for a while...

Jesus silenced devils because they were speaking the truth about Him at a time when He was trying to conceal His identity from most people.

Also, note the actions of these devils in a man:

> *And they came over unto the other side of the sea, into the country of the Gadarenes.*
> *And when He was come out of the ship, immediately there met Him out of the tombs a man with an unclean spirit, who had his dwelling among the tombs; and no man could bind him, no, not with chains: Because that he had been often bound with fetters and chains, and the chains had been plucked asunder by him, and the fetters broken in pieces: neither could any man tame him.*
> *And always, night and day, he was in the mountains, and in the tombs, crying, and cutting himself with stones.*
> *But when he saw Jesus afar off,* **he ran AND WORSHIPPED HIM,** *And cried with a loud voice, and said,* **WHAT HAVE I TO DO WITH THEE, JESUS, THOU SON OF THE MOST HIGH GOD? I adjure Thee by God, that Thou torment me not.**
> *For He said unto him, Come out of the man, thou unclean spirit.*
> *And He asked him, What is thy name?*
> *And he answered, saying, My name is Legion: for we are many.* ~ Mark 5:1-9

Please do not overlook that a demonized man, who could not be bound with chains and fetters, ran to Jesus, and bowed down to worship Him. When Samson demonstrated his feats of strength, it was because the Holy Spirit had empowered him. Likewise, that man's strength was from the devils that were in him. Yet, he could run to Jesus and worship/bow down before Him. That man was not the only person who was worshipping the LORD. IF only by default, so were those devils who were pleading with the LORD. But, according to the Scripture, the actions of the man and the words from his lips were those of the devils within him.

Those devils were truthful about Jesus's identity and authority. Their time IS rapidly coming to an end, which factors into why even due to desperation, devils will tell the truth at times. But they WILL receive their rewards from the LORD Jesus Christ, along with every other messenger of Satan for their evil deeds. Job made this commentary after Satan afflicted him, twice:

For the thing which I greatly feared is come upon me, and that which I was afraid of is come unto me.
~ Job 3:25

The thing that Satan and his messengers fear, the lake of fire and brimstone, will soon come upon them. The LORD will stop simply casting devils out of people because He will permanently cast them into a place of everlasting torments, where they will be engulfed in the unending flames of the lake of fire and brimstone.

CHAPTER 5
THE DEVIL

Not only CAN the Devil tell the truth, but there is a time when he MUST tell the truth. That is where the duality of his nature and purpose reaches its fullness. In Revelation 12, Lucifer is referred to as Satan and the Devil. Basically, Satan is the serpent who seduces people to sin, and the Devil is the dragon who accuses people of sin before God (day and night). When witnesses are sworn into a court in the United States, they are asked if they will tell "the truth, the whole truth, and nothing but the truth." People do not always adhere to the "Witness Oath/Affirmation" because they may falsely claim they cannot recall certain things, even when they can. The judge may also choose to exclude certain evidence from consideration. But those things do not work in God's court. The Devil cannot go before God to accuse His children based on lies. The Devil can speculate, such as in Job 1-2, when he speculated that Job would curse God to His face if He removed His hedge of protection from Job so that he, the Devil, could afflict him. The LORD allowed Satan to test his theories against Job, and they failed miserably. But a part of God allowing that was to foreshadow how His Son, Jesus the

Christ, would suffer at the hands of the Devil, despite His innocence, and He would not curse His Father either, despite lamenting about His sufferings.

When the Devil accuses a child of God, to God, it must be with the truth. The Devil may not tell the whole truth, such as the conditions he crafted to (potentially) ensnare the child of God, but he will and must tell the truth about how the child of God responded to his seduction. For example, when David saw a woman cleaning herself and was enticed by her. There is no Scriptural evidence that she was trying to seduce the king, but it represents how Satan entices us to sin. King David inquired about the woman's identity and found out that she was Bathsheba, the wife of one of his top thirty men, Uriah the Hittite. A Scripture from the New Testament states:

> *There hath no temptation taken you but such as is common to man:* **but God is faithful, who will not suffer you to be tempted above that ye are able; BUT WILL WITH THE TEMPTATION ALSO MAKE A WAY TO ESCAPE, that ye may be able to bear it.**
> ~ 1 Corinthians 10:13

That is part of why the enemy attacks CHRISTians with sinful dreams of things they will not engage in during their waking moments. But that is to his condemnation, and such things, based on Leviticus 6:1-7, will not withstand God's cross-examination. Also, those covert attacks are attempts to pluck the LORD's sheep from His hand, which will not work either (John 10:28-29).

When David learned the identity and marital status of the naked woman he saw from his roof, especially for a king with several wives and concubines, that was the way of escape the LORD had given to him. Sadly, instead of taking that opportunity to flee from sexual immorality, King David took Bathsheba, which opened the door to a multitude of sins and havoc in his life and family (2 Samuel 11). But when the Prophet Nathan came to impose God's judgment upon the king, he knew the prophet was telling the truth. It represented the Devil having had a solid case against him, and rather than trying to say God and/or the Devil was wrong, David confessed to his sins. The LORD responded to David's actions by still judging him, but with mercy due to his confession. The consequences for King David were grave, but the LORD spared his life (2 Samuel 12:7-15).

Those are the types of charges the Devil wants to bring against us to God: cases where we are guilty as sin, as the saying goes. In such situations, we are best served by admitting our guilt and throwing ourselves at God's feet for mercy. But if the Devil uses lies, he and his accusations would get thrown out, faster than lightning. Even Satan must pass the bar by not violating the LORD's Commandment not to bear false witness (Exodus 20:16).

I can attest, and perhaps so can you, that one of the worst feelings is when a devil seduces you to do something, and sometimes, as soon as you take his bait, you feel instant regret. That is when he bombards you with feelings of worthlessness and that it may be best to end your own life. And to add insult to injury, you know the devil is correct when he confronts you in your sins. The Bible has an example of this when the prophet from Bethel misled the prophet from Judah to sin against God. Shockingly, instead of the LORD rebuking the Judean directly, He had the Bethelite do it, even though he was the one who lied and caused the Judean to sin (1 Kings 13:11-32).

On the contrary, if his attacks are fabricated, such as in a dream or vision, you can boldly appear before the throne of grace and ask the LORD to judge between you and those who are trying to entice you to sin, or, worse, make you sin against God.

A part of why the enemy attacks while you sleep is to sow seeds of sin, such as trying to remind you of how pleasurable it was to engage in those sins. The attacks confirm that what God said to Cain is true, that sin is a person, and in your case, that person is trying to get back into your life to dominate you.

If the Devil wants to stand a chance with you before God, he must get you to sin somehow so he can accuse you to God with the truth. When he attacks in dreams, his intention is to get you to engage in those things in your waking moments. It is a cruel form of entrapment from a SINister person, but regardless of what he tries while you sleep, you must rule over sin. You are NEVER obligated to keep any covenants the Devil tries to make with you, especially when he does so covertly [see Isaiah 28:18 and 2 Corinthians 6:14-18].

Surprisingly, one of the worst things a person can do is to falsely accuse the enemy of making them sin. If he had a role, that is one thing, but we must be careful that we do not use Satan as a scapegoat for our actions. Please keep this important lesson in mind:

*Yet Michael the archangel, when contending with the Devil he disputed about the body of Moses, durst not bring against him a **railing accusation**, but said, The* L*ORD rebuke thee.* ~ Jude 1:9

Another term for railing accusation is blasphemy [against the Devil]. Instead of falsely blaming the Devil for your actions, repent and seek the LORD for His mercy; do not shift blame unjustly.

Jesus is a merciful, fair, and firm Judge. Technically speaking, anyone who goes to hell can get tossed directly into the lake of fire and brimstone and justice would be served. But death and hell will have to give up the dead which are in them, and to give them due process; they will stand before the LORD Jesus Christ for judgment (Revelation 20:11-15). However, even though the Devil has served as a prosecutor of God's children by bringing charges against them before God, he will be disbarred. Satan will not accuse people in the end. Additionally, he will not defend his servants, but he would not, even if he could, because he will be incarcerated and therefore incapacitated:

And the Devil that deceived them was cast into the lake of fire and brimstone, where the beast and the false prophet are, and shall be tormented day and night for ever and ever. ~ Revelation 20:10

EPILOGUE

Satan is a liar and the father of lies, and he will go where all liars do, which is the lake of fire and brimstone (Revelation 21:8). But while he is free to lie with impunity, if he is going to accuse you of being a sinner before God, he must tell the truth, or he will be bearing false witness against you. When the Devil truthfully accuses you of sin, that is when you will realize how well devils know the Word of God, but that they are hypocrites who do not live by it. That knowledge is a necessity because, in whichever way possible, they try to get you to sin by violating God's Words. Hence, we need the Spirit of God and God's grace through His Son, Jesus the Christ.

When I read this Scripture, it is a part of my prayer that it includes the Devil, for him to join everyone in professing this Truth:

*Wherefore God also hath highly exalted Him, and given Him a name which is above every name: That at the name of Jesus **every knee should bow**, of things in heaven, and things in earth, and things under the earth; And that **every tongue should confess** that **JESUS CHRIST IS LORD**, to the glory of God the Father.*
~ Philippians 2:9-11

I sincerely pray that Satan, also known as the Devil, will be the first one to bow before Jesus and truthfully make this confession:

Jesus Christ is LORD!

If he thought having Jesus crucified was embarrassing to the LORD and those who bore witness of the crucifixion, I think it would be poetic justice to have Satan do that before all creation, as he leads the chant that Jesus

Christ is LORD! It would be like what King Ahasuerus/Xerxes had Haman do to Mordecai. Haman had plotted to have Mordecai killed, but instead, he had to lead the procession and have others honor the Jew in Persia. I hope that when Satan read that Scripture, he considered the possibility that it foreshadowed what the Father would have him do to honor His Son, Jesus Christ. The Man he sought to crucify is the One he must later glorify; then he can go down to the pit, sulking as Haman did after having to parade Mordecai through the streets (Esther 6).

All hail the KING of Kings and the LORD of Lords, Jesus the Christ, the Son of the True and the Living God!

ABOUT THE AUTHOR

Kollin L. Taylor is a Jamaican-born American combat veteran of natural and spiritual battles. The LORD Jesus Christ called Kollin to "Minister to the people." He fulfills that mandate in a multitude of ways, such as through the following published books:

- *Exposed Part 1: The Prelude*
- *Exposed Part 2: Romantic Relationships*
- *Exposed Part 3: Vida*
- *Exposed Part 4: The Journey Continues*
- *Metamorphosis: The New Me*
- *The Phenom: From My Soul*
- *The Aftermath: When the Smoke Clears and the Dust Settles*
- *Resilience: Bend, Don't Break*
- *Perspective: A New Point of View*
- *The Anatomy of a Heartbreak: When SAMson Met Delilah*
- *Round 2: The Battle Continues*
- *Round 3: Still Fighting*
- *Cool Breeze: Irie Man!*
- *Finding Joy in YOU: The Gift of Eternal Life*
- *The Path to Enlightenment*
- *Minister to the People: Answering His Calling*
- *Australia: A Journey Down Under*
- *Wrongfully Accused: When Innocence Is Not Enough*
- *The Sidelines: Those Who Can...*

When Satan Tells the Truth

- *Flirting with Disaster*
- *The Sound of a Fallen Tree*
- *Survival*
- *Humble Pie: A Gift from God*
- *Second Chance: Worthy of Redemption*
- *God's Kitchen: His Slow-Cooked Stew*
- *God, the Love of my Life*
- *God Speaks to My Soul*
- *On Trial: A Test of My Faith*
- *Closet Christian: If You Deny Him, He Will Deny You*
- *Soul Food: Thanks Lord, for My Daily Bread*
- *Knowledge is Power: Before You Do What You're Told, Know What You're Being Told*
- *Labor Pains... Waiting to Push!*
- *Breakthrough: When Jesus Sets You Free*
- *Born Again: Renew Your Mind with the Holy Spirit*
- *Holy Spirit Led: My Steps are Ordered*
- *Raised in the Wilderness: Rogue Reformers, Rallying the Remnant*
- *So, You Want to be a Prophet... ARE YOU CRAZY?*
- *The Process: The Refiner's Fire*
- *So, You Want to Marry a Prophet... ARE YOU CRAZY?*
- *The Prophet and the witch: Under the Influence*
- *The Devil's War Against Your God-Ordained Marriage*
- *The Blind Seer: Seeing in the Dark*
- *Psalmists Arise: Beyond the Music*
- *Intercessory Birth Pangs: The Prophetic Intercessor*

- *The Watchman: What Do You See?*
- *Apostolic Authority: Unleashing Heaven on Hell*
- *Child Soldier: Train Up a Child for [Spiritual] Warfare*
- *RelationWITCH: Godly Wait or the devil's Bait*
- *Apostle in Training: Suffering Shame for Jesus's Name*
- *It May Be DEMONic AND You Need Deliverance IF…The Life of a Tormented Christian*
- *Roles & Responsibilities for Today's Prophets (of the Lord)*
- *FOUR Shades of Prophets: The Slippery Slope to Hell*
- *The Prophet's Life: Prophetic fACTS, Prophetic Acts*
- *The Enigmatic Evangelist: Heaven's Delta Force*
- *Good God: Why God Allows Suffering*
- *Discern or Burn: Let No One Deceive You*
- *Redeeming the Fallen Prophet: The Road to Restoration*
- *Loving You, My Enemy: A Guide to Pray for Your Persecutors*
- ***When Satan Tells the Truth: Sweet Little Lies***

Author Photo
(self-portrait)